GORILLAS

A PORTRAIT OF THE ANIMAL WORLD

JILL M. CARAVAN

TODTRI

This book was designed and produced by
TODTRI Book Publishers
P.O. Box 572, New York, NY 10116-0572
FAX: (212) 695-6984
e-mail: info@todtri.com

Printed and bound in Singapore

ISBN 1-57717-133-0

Author: Jill M. Caravan

Publisher: Robert M. Tod
Senior Editor: Edward Douglas
Photo Editor: Linda Waldman
Book Designer: Mark Weinberg
Typesetting: Command-O, NYC

Visit us on the web!
www.todtri.com

PHOTO CREDITS

Photo Source/Page Number

Karl Amman, 3, 7, 12 (bottom), 13, 14, 15 (left), 16 (top), 18, 23, 24–25, 28, 31,
43, 45 (bottom right), 46, 50 (top), 53, 63 (bottom), 64, 69 (bottom)

Walt Anderson, 29, 34 (top), 35, 37, 38 (top & bottom), 48, 52

Peter Arnold, Inc.
Y. Arthus-Bertrand, 58
Compost/Visage, 12 (top), 69 (top)
M.&C. Denis-Huot, 34 (bottom)
M. Gunther, 60, 62
Günther Ziesler, 26 (bottom)

Martha Hill/Kevin Schafer, 61 (top)

Joe McDonald, 5, 11 (top), 47

National Geographic Society
Michael Nichols, 4, 6, 8–9, 11 (bottom), 16 (bottom), 20, 26 (top), 27, 30 (top & bottom), 32, 33, 36, 39, 40–41,
45 (top right), 49, 50 (bottom), 51, 55, 56–57, 61 (bottom), 63 (top), 65, 66 (top), 67, 68, 70 (bottom)
Peter G. Veit, 66 (bottom)

Picture Perfect, 19

Kevin Schafer, 10, 15 (right), 17, 21, 22, 54, 59, 70 (top), 71

Art Wolfe, 42, 44–45

INTRODUCTION

This silverback in Zaire's Virunga National Park silently chews on a stem, demonstrating that gorillas are usually quite silent, the gentle giants of the animal world.

A lifelong resident of eastern Pennsylvania, I have made many visits to the Philadelphia Zoo—on class trips, scout trips, or just as a family activity. I always look forward to seeing all the animals at the zoo, of course, but even as an adult, the highlight for me has always been visiting the primates—especially the gorillas. Thinking of those visits, I realize the reason we all must be drawn to the primates is that they remind us so much of ourselves.

For many reasons, I think we feel most akin to the gorillas. Scientifically, they share 99 percent of humans' genetic makeup: they have forty-eight chromosomes, we have forty-six. They have two legs and two arms, ten fingers and ten toes, small ears on the side of the head, forward-facing eyes, and thirty-two teeth. Their skulls are also similar to human skulls. Male gorillas are about the size of male humans—five and a half to six feet (1.7–1.8 m)—and from a distance could be mistaken for humans. They use their hands to pick and prepare their own food. They eat together and they sleep together. They live in family groups and protect each other. Infants nurse from and stay with their mothers for the first few years. They play with each other and with their parents, not just running and climbing, but even creating games with round fruit and other vegetation. As they grow up, they go through a kind of puberty, in which they are not quite mature, but are allowed to go out on their own and explore. The young males form groups and search out females—not unlike human teenagers. Gorillas have facial expressions that tell us if they are happy, sad, or upset. They laugh when they are tickled. Dian Fossey once even observed a three– or four-year-old gorilla shed tears, when the orphaned gorilla Coco looked

out into the forest from a room in Fossey's cabin, after being rescued from poachers.

Maybe all these similarities help explain why we are not surprised to learn that another gorilla named Koko (spelled with Ks instead of Cs) was able to learn to communicate using sign language, or why we coo when we see a gorilla in a movie or on television holding a gorilla infant or a kitten, or rescuing a human toddler that fell into its enclosure, or why we wept when twenty-three primates, including gorillas, were killed in a 1995 fire at the World of Primates exhibit at the Philadelphia Zoo.

As this book is being written, the Philadelphia Zoo is involved in reconstruction of a two-and-a-half-acre Primate Reserve. We still mourn for the gorillas we came to know and love in the old exhibit, but look forward to the day when we can visit gorillas there again.

We also weep for the many gorillas who have died and continue to die at the hands of humans, as a result of activities such as poaching, war, and habitat destruction for tourism, farming, and development.

We know that gorillas are animals. After all, they are almost totally covered in fur, do not have human hygiene habits, and prefer to sleep outside. But as we watch their behavior and look into their eyes, we see something more.

Because gorillas like Koko show us that they can be almost human—from signing, to laughing, to lying, to loving and grieving—we realize that they are just one step away from being the best of what is human about us.

The upright stance is usually used for chestbeating with open, cupped hands—not fists—in order to warn, show off, or just because it feels good.

PHYSICAL CHARACTERISTICS

Scientists do not know exactly how long gorillas have existed, but a Roman explorer is believed to be the first person in Western civilization ever to see a gorilla, in the year 5 B.C. Given our current theories of evolution, it makes sense that relatives of the gorilla (primates) have been recorded on fossils that are dated at about seventy million years ago. Fossils also show that relatives of apes diverged from the primate line about twenty million years ago. Several million years ago the chimpanzee and gorilla lines had already separated from each other, and the orangutan line even earlier than that.

The Primates

Throughout the eighteenth century there remained a considerable amount of confusion in distinguishing between orangutans, chimpanzees, and gorillas. Because of its remote habitat in Asia, the orangutan was the first to be recognized as a distinct genus. Not until 1847, on the basis of a single skull from Gabon, was the gorilla confirmed as a separate genus from the chimpanzee, although fossil records and biochemical research show that chimpanzees are the gorillas' closest relative.

In the eighteenth century Carl Linnaeus, the first serious student of classification, devised a system that classified animals first by class, order, and family, then genus and species. Like all animals classed as mammals, gorillas are warm-blooded, have hair, are nursed by mother's milk, and go through a rather long childhood. Humans, whales, elephants, dolphins, horses, cats, monkeys, and apes are all part of the mammal class. In 1758 Linnaeus officially recognized the close relationship between humans, monkeys, and apes and devised the order name primate to encompass them all and to denote their high ranking in the animal kingdom. The primate order contains eleven families, including lemurs,

FOLLOWING PAGE: Gorillas use their hands to collect and prepare their food, to carry their young, to play, and to build nests. Some gorillas in captivity have even been taught to communicate, using the hand signals of American Sign Language, developed for the hearing impaired.

Male gorillas average 5 1/2 feet (1.7 m) and 400 pounds (182 kg), and can spread their arms about 8 feet (2.4 m) across. They can reach 6 feet (1.8 m) in height and 500 pounds (227 kg) in weight.

Gorillas, like other mammals, are warm blooded, are covered with fur or hair, are nursed by mother's milk, and have a rather long childhood. Other mammals include humans, whales, elephants, dolphins, lemurs, monkeys, marmosets, great apes, and many other kinds of creatures.

monkeys, apes, marmosets, great apes, and humans. Gorillas are members of the family Hominidae, the great apes. None of the great apes are considered direct ancestors of humans, (*Homo sapiens*), but they do share enough close physical characteristics with humans to provide us with clues about the behavior of our ancestors.

There are now 230 species of primate. The great apes are the largest, and gorillas are the largest of the four great apes; the others are the chimpanzee, bonobo (or pygmy chimpanzee), and organutan. Gibbons and siamangs are known as lesser apes. According to Linnaeus, humans and apes are the only primates without tails and, like most primates, have five digits on each hand and foot, the first of which is opposable. Anatomical features of all primates are two mammae (nipples); usually a total of thirty-two teeth; and eyes directed forward to permit binocular vision (both eyes seeing together), since they depend greatly on eyesight to gather food and avoid predators. Primates are omnivorous (eating both plants and meat), although many who live in rain forests are more vegetarian (plant-eating) than carnivorous (meat-eating). They live in trees and range in size from the two-

The chimpanzee is the gorilla's closest relative, according to fossil records and biochemical research. It was confirmed as a separate species in 1847.

The bonobo is among the apes that, along with man, are the only primates without tails and, like most primates, have five digits on each hand and foot, the first of which is opposable. The others are orangutan, chimpanzee, gorilla, and gibbon.

In Malay "orang" means "person" and "hutan" means "forest," thus orangutan means "person of the forest." The indigenous, or native, people of Borneo consider orangutans to be another tribe or people, thus the name orangutan.

The orangutan was once found throughout Southeast Asia, but today survives only on the islands of Borneo and Sumatra. Recent estimates suggest the population could be as low as 15,000 to 20,000.

ounce (5.7 g) mouse lemur to the 400-pound (182 kg) gorilla.

Orangutans, gibbons, and siamangs inhabit Asia, but the natural habitat of gorillas, chimpanzees, and bonobos is Africa. Gorillas live in the rain forests and the densely wooded areas of two African regions, equatorial west Africa and east central Africa, which are separated by the 622 miles (1,000 km) of the Congo Basin tropical forest. Large rivers probably act as geographical barriers between the western and eastern populations of gorillas. Favored gorilla habitats are forest edges, regenerating (secondary) forest, montane forest, riverine forest, bamboo forest in certain seasons, and in lower numbers in primary forest at low density.

In recent history, the first outsider to see the mountain gorilla was a German, Captain Oscar von Beringei. In October 1902, while traveling across eastern Africa, he observed some tall manlike apes on one of the volcanoes of the Virunga region of Ruanda-Urundi (now Rwanda). He was also the first European to shoot a mountain gorilla. The gorilla subspecies *Gorilla gorilla beringei* was later named after him. Not until the mid-twentieth century was the first scientific expedition attempted to study the gorillas in their natural habitat.

These tall, manlike apes are what Captain Oscar von Berengei saw on top of the volcanoes of the Virunga region of Rwanda when he was traveling across eastern Africa in 1902. He was the first outsider in recent history to see the mountain gorilla.

Bonobos are known to make more facial expressions than almost any other primates, including the habit of covering their eyes and walking around blind.

Subspecies

The three subspecies of gorilla are distinguished by their physical differences and their distribution in Africa: the western lowland gorilla (*Gorilla gorilla gorilla*), the eastern lowland gorilla (*G. g. graueri*), and the very rare mountain gorilla (*G. g. beringei*). While the three differ geographically, they are very similar morphologically (structurally). Any adaptations are related to their individual habitats. Research as recent as 1994 resulted in the theory that there are actually only two subspecies, but most organizations concerned about gorillas still list three.

The western lowland gorilla, the smallest of the subspecies, with short blackish hair (sometimes reddish-brown on the head), is found in western Africa: southeast Nigeria, Cameroon, equatorial Guinea, Gabon, Congo (Brazzaville), and the forested areas of the Central African Republic. Its easternmost range is the Oubangui River. A wide gap exists between this large area of distribution and the two other subspecies, each with extremely limited ranges. The western lowland gorilla inhabits tropical rain forests, forest edges and clearings, riverine forests, swamps, and abandoned cultivated fields. While preliminary studies placed western lowland gorillas in sunny, dry secondary growth or open forests where dense vegetation thrives, recent field work revealed that these gorillas use all forest types, including swampy areas, for nesting and feeding. These are the gorillas usually seen in zoos and mounted in museums. About 600 exist in captivity around the world (just over 300 in North America),

Sitting calmly in the grass, this male lowland gorilla looks quite human-like, exhibiting the same two legs and arms, ten fingers and ten toes, small ears on the side of the head, forward-facing eyes, thirty-two teeth, and a similar skull shape.

The Zaire River splits the wild habitats of the 5,000 to 10,000 eastern lowland gorillas and the less than 10,000 western lowland gorillas. In captivity there are less than two dozen eastern gorillas and approximately 600 western gorillas.

Finding an adequate source of mealtime vegetation is such serious business that this gorilla and his group will brave swampland to find food. Gorillas generally prefer forest land and tend to avoid water.

About 330 mountain gorillas live in the Virunga Volcano region, with its characteristic mist. The area was previously connected to the Bwinda forest, habitat for about 320 gorillas, but agriculture has separated the two areas.

Most gorillas, like these mountain gorillas at the Karisoke Research Center in Rwanda, live mostly on the ground, so their short trunks and outsized arms that served their tree-dwelling ancestors are no longer necessary.

and fewer than 100,000 are thought to be left in the wild.

The eastern lowland gorilla ranges from Zaire to the west of Lake Tanganyika and Lake Edward, from the lower altitudes of 2,500–7,400 feet (762–2255 m). This gorilla has shorter hair like the western lowland gorilla, with a narrower face and broader chest than its western cousin, but is slightly larger. Fewer than two dozen exist in captivity (among these are three in Antwerp, Belgium, and one in Houston, Texas). Only 5,000 to 10,000 are thought to be left in the wild.

The mountain gorilla is found about 1,000 miles (1609 km) east of the western lowland gorilla, from the Virunga Volcanoes and the Bwindi Forest at altitudes of 5,400 to 13,000 feet (1646–3962 m), on the Zaire-Rwanda border and in Uganda. Mountain gorillas are found in montane, riverine, or bamboo forest zones that are lush and moist, and provide an abundance of forage at ground level year round. The mountain gorilla is the largest of the subspecies and its hair is the longest, providing warmth in the gorilla's cool and damp mountainous habitat.

This female mountain gorilla feels at home in vegetation. Most primates are omnivorous (eating plants and meat), although many who live in rain forests are more herbivorous (plant-eating) than carnivorous (meat-eating).

With the exception of dependent babies, all gorillas generally build nests for themselves in which to sleep at night, but most are rather more sanitary than those of the Virungas, where conditions may be quite frigid. The gorillas from this area defecate in their nests and sleep on their dung, because, it is believed, the dry and rather fibrous dung makes a good insulator in the extreme cold.

Mountain gorillas are the rarest of the gorillas, with fewer than 600–650 left in the wild and none in captivity. The wild population is restricted to two small groups, about 330 in the Virunga Volcano region, and about 320 in the Bwinda forest. In the past these two areas were connected by forest, but as the local human population grew, the forests were cut down and the areas are now surrounded and separated by about 15 miles (24 km) of agriculture. The rare mountain gorilla is the species that scientists—most notably Dian Fossey, author of *Gorillas in the Mist*—studied in Rwanda.

Anatomy

Gorillas look something like stocky, midsized men: a being you wouldn't want to oppose in a wrestling match, especially since they can be as strong as four to eight men. Males average five and a half feet (1.7 m) and 400 pounds (182 kg), but can be more than 6 feet tall (1.8 m) and weigh up to 500 pounds (227 kg). They can spread their arms about eight feet (2.4 m) across. Females average about a foot (.3 m) shorter than males and are about half as heavy: four and a half feet tall (1.4 m) and 200 pounds (91 kg). *Gorilla graueris* are the largest, averaging five feet nine inches (1.75 m) and 360 pounds (163 kg); *Gorilla beringei*, five feet eight inches (1.73 m), 343 pounds (156 kg); and *Gorilla gorilla*, five feet six inches (1.7 m), 307 pounds (139 kg).

Gorillas have broad chests topped by massive heads, with protruding foreheads and a pointy crest on top, usually more noticeable in adult males. Their eyes, generally small and close-set, are usually dark brown. Their relatively

The eyes of a gorilla are generally small, close-set, and dark brown. Gorillas appear to be nearsighted because they hold food and other items close to their eyes to focus on them but can detect movement at a distance.

Researchers have used gorillas' distinct nose prints to identify individual gorillas, along with the shape of their face: round or oval, flat or bulging.

small ears lie close to the skull. Noses can vary, but are generally what humans consider to be "apelike," with flared nostrils. The western lowland gorilla has an overhanging tip on its nose that distinguishes it from the eastern. Researchers have used gorillas' distinct nose prints to identify individual gorillas. Along with nose shape, they can sometimes be identified by the shape of their face: round or oval, flat or bulging.

Like humans, gorillas have thirty-two teeth, but the great apes' teeth far outrank those of humans in strength. The male's canines are much larger than the female's. To process a tremendous amount of vegetation, the molars are very large. That diet also requires enlarged intestines, making gorillas appear pot-bellied.

Gorillas have short trunks and outsized arms, longer than their legs. The lengthy arms served gorillas' tree-dwelling ancestors, but now they are just oversized, since today's gorillas live mostly on the ground. But the short, stubby opposable "thumbs" on those arms (and the big toe on the feet) are one of the

Gorillas have five digits on each hand and foot, the first of which is opposable, which enables them to maneuver and hold onto objects, prepare food, and make their nests each night.

features that put them in a category with humans, enabling them to hold and manipulate objects, like humans do, although they are not known to use tools.

Despite their humanlike characteristics, gorillas usually use all four limbs to walk, curling up their fingers and knuckle-walking with their arms and stretching up on the soles of their feet. They are capable of walking on just their legs, but are not known to do this for more than about 20 feet (6 m). The upright stance is usually used for chestbeating, to observe something, or to reach an object

Gorillas' skin is dark, covered with bluish-black to reddish-brown or grayish-brown hair, except on the face, chest, underarms, palms of hands, fingers, and soles of the feet. As they age, the hair turns gray, and thins out on the chests of males. At sexual maturity, usually around age eleven, males acquire silver-gray saddles across their backs and upper thighs, hence the name silverback, usually reserved for the dominant male of a group. The male western lowland gorilla's saddle is grayish or brownish, extends to the thighs, and is not sharply defined. In the eastern lowland gorilla, the fur is fairly short; in the mountain gorilla, long and silky.

No one knows for certain how long gorillas live in the wild, but scientists estimate their life span at about thirty-five years, although they have been known to live more than fifty. The in-captivity record was set by Massa in the Philadelphia Zoo, who lived fifty-four years and one day. In the wild, the mortality rate for immature gorillas under age six is more than 40 percent, and the risks are highest during the first year. Fighting silverbacks,

Gorillas usually use all four limbs to walk, curling up their fingers to knuckle-walk with their arms while stretching up on the soles of their feet. They can walk on just their legs, but are not known to do this for more than about 20 feet (6 m).

predation, injury, and disease are all serious threats to youngsters that lessen as the apes reach maturity, though the risks continue throughout life.

Senses

Although gorillas' senses have not been studied extensively, their senses of smell, sight, and hearing appear to be good. The animals seem to respond well to noises, both those generating from within and from outside the group. And they are able to hear danger and each other when trying to locate group members among the vegetation. They can locate each other by smell, and are able to detect the scent of another gorilla or a human that might pose danger for the group. They also can tell a female's reproductive status by her scent.

Gorillas appear to be what humans call nearsighted; they must hold food and other items close to their eyes to focus on them. But they manage quite well to find and identify food, perhaps even being able to see colors to know if fruit has ripened. They can also detect movement by sight.

FOLLOWING PAGE: This family portrait of bonobos shows one of the four great apes. Among their distinguishing characteristics are the lack of a tail and their great dependence on eyesight to gather food and avoid predators.

A young orangutan usually remains with its mother for eight years, learning to become an expert forager by observing her methods of finding and processing food. In eight hours an orangutan can consume all the edible produce on one tree.

The orangutan, one of the great apes, was thought to be indistinguishable from the gorilla and the chimpanzee throughout the eighteenth century. It was the first to be recognized as a distinct genus because of its remote Asian habitat.

This pygmy chimpanzee, catching ants on a stick, belongs to a primate species that hunts, kills, and eats other animals. Although gorillas do eat insects, they favor sugary fruits, low-fat unripe seeds, fibrous plant stems, and protein-rich new leaves.

The demeanor of this chimpanzee alpha male is much the same as a silverback gorilla that has charge of his group. The genetic code of both chimps and gorillas is 98.6 and 97.7 percent human.

This 24-year-old mountain gorilla named Mrithi led a twelve-member family before his accidental death by automatic assault weapons in Rwanda's Parc National des Volvans. He was also featured in Gorillas in the Mist, *the movie about Dian Fossey's intense work with these animals.*

GORILLA BEHAVIOR

Gorillas are pack animals, meaning that, like canines (dogs and wolves), they live in groups called bands. The groups range in size from two to forty, but average six or seven, and are led by a dominant male (silverback), the most experienced and knowledgeable gorilla in the group. The rest of the group consists of several mature females and their young of various ages, including maturing males and females. Bonds between the silverback and each female hold the group together, and everyone has a place in it.

The Pack Leader

In his role as leader, the silverback protects the females and young gorillas from predators and other male gorillas. He also has prerogative to sexual access to the breeding females. But the younger males work with him to protect the group as guards and lookouts.

Because bonobos substitute sex for aggression, sexual interactions occur more frequently among bonobos than among other primates, and in almost any partnership combination.

The silverback is the most experienced and knowledgeable gorilla in the group. The rest of the group is composed of several mature females and their young of various ages, including maturing males and females.

As the young males (blackbacks) mature, they leave the band or are driven off by the silverback, usually as a result of competition for the females. Sometimes they converge into what are called bachelor groups until they find available females with which to form new bands. One of these wandering males may lure mature females away from their group to start a new group. This assures that there is no inbreeding among a group.

There is usually a dominant female, who is the silverback's favorite. Her size is not a factor in her dominance, but rather her personality and experience. A female rises in the "ranks" as she has offspring, and those females who have not had babies rank the lowest.

Gorillas are pack animals, meaning, like canines (dogs and wolves), they live in groups called "bands." The groups range in size from two to forty, but average six or seven, and are led by a dominant male

Titus, the leader of this family group, resting at the Karisoke Research Center, Rwanda, is charged with protecting the females and young gorillas from predators and other male gorillas.

Breeding occurs when one gorilla manages to get another gorilla's attention during the female's period of ovulation. There is usually a dominant female, who is the silverback's favorite.

Sleeping and Eating Habits

The group spends most of its days feeding (about 30 percent), sleeping (about 40 percent), traveling, grooming, and playing, all at a leisurely pace and all decided by the silverback. Like humans, gorillas are diurnal, active during the day and sleeping at night.

Rising with the dawn, they start the day eating and continue eating as they proceed through their day: moving a bit, resting awhile, moving some more, and then at sunset

Trailing vegetation provides a source of food and a comfortable seat for this young mountain gorilla in the Karisoke Research Center. Though separated, the gorillas can locate each other by smell as well as sight.

resting again. All gorillas build a nest for their nighttime rest, and some may even do so for the midday siesta. These nests are built for only one night's use, with whatever materials are on hand, usually grasses, leaves, and branches. The materials are bent or woven into the shape of a circular, springy bowl, about three and a half feet (1 m) in diameter. (Chimpanzees build nests the same way, but usually higher in the trees.) The heavier gorillas (including silverbacks) build their nests in low-to-the-ground vegetation or on the ground, and the lighter members of the group build theirs highest in the vegetation and even up in the trees. This may be a function of protection as well as weight, since the heavier gorillas would be more likely to fend off any attackers. Infants up to about age three sleep with their mothers.

All gorillas build nests to sleep in during the night, but after traveling and eating throughout the day they may take a more spontaneous midday siesta, without a nest.

Like humans, gorillas are diurnal (active during the day and sleeping at night) but nothing feels better than catching a nap in the sun after a good meal during the day.

For the feeding portion of the day, gorillas choose from more than two hundred selections on a true vegetarian menu: herbs, vines, fruits, leaves, stems, bamboo, bark, flowers, wood, fungi, and occasionally invertebrates (insects such as termites and ants, or snails and slugs), using their hands and mouth to collect and prepare the food. Gorillas live mainly on the ground, but whole groups have been seen up in the stronger trees when they are fruiting. Even silverbacks have been known to climb as high as 90 feet (27 m).

Analysis of gorilla dung has shown that the animals favor sugary fruits, low-fat unripe seeds, fibrous plant stems, and protein-rich new leaves. They rarely need to drink water because their plant diet has such a high water content. Each band favors a certain area within its range, and follows a seasonal pattern depending upon what fruits are ripe at what time of year. Unlike their cousins the chimpanzees, gorillas do not hunt, kill, or eat other animals. When fruits are scarce, gorillas, also unlike chimpanzees, can switch to a coarser diet of ground plants. Since gorillas don't stay very long at any one particular feeding site, they never completely deplete their food source.

Because gorillas spend much of their day feeding, they move from place to place, and may travel from a quarter to a half mile (.4–.8 km) per day. However, once they have covered about 2 to 15 square miles (5–40 sq km), they stay within that range. The area that each band uses remains fairly exclusive to it, but unlike their chimpanzee cousins, there is no overt territoriality among the bands. In fact, neighboring bands may sometimes overlap territories.

Thirty percent of a gorilla's day is spent feeding, with 40 percent devoted to sleeping. The rest of the time is spent traveling, grooming, and playing. All the day's activities are decided by the silverback.

Because gorillas spend much of their day feeding, they move from place to place, and may travel up to 1/2 mile (.8 km) per day. However, once they have covered about 2 to 15 square miles (5 to 40 sq. km), they stay within that range

Reproduction and Development

Breeding is not confined to any particular time of year, but rather occurs when one gorilla manages to get another gorilla's attention, during the female's period of ovulation. Female gorillas reach sexual maturity (perineal swelling) at about age eight to ten, but generally do not conceive for the first time until age ten to twelve. When a female is receptive, with perineal swelling about two days a month, she will solicit the attention of the silverback or another male with special glances and touches.

Males become adult in most respects at about age eight, after which they go through a "blackback" period. Although sexually mature, they are not socially mature, do not lead groups, and may live on their own sometimes. However, like human teenagers, they retain their playful nature and maintain a fairly close relationship with the leading silverback. They begin getting their "silverbacks" at age eleven to thirteen, but they do not automatically strike out on their own at that stage and normally do not breed until closer to age fifteen to twenty, especially because there is so much competition for females.

The gorilla's reproductive rate is quite low. The females breed only once every four to eight years. They produce only one baby, and approximately half the babies die in the first year of life or before reaching sexual maturity, because of injury, illness, or dependency on the mother, which also faces these risks. In her lifetime, a mother usually raises about three infants to maturity.

Once breeding has been completed, the "couple" must wait about 258 days (about eight and a half to nine months) for their new offspring. Infant gorillas weigh three to five pounds (1.4–2.3 kg) at birth. Newborns have pinkish-gray skin, which darkens within a few weeks to jet black, and are sparsely covered with fur. They may have a white patch on their rumps for the first few years. Although they develop twice as fast as human babies, they stay with their mothers for two to three years, nursing much of the time. They are introduced to solid foods at about six months.

Males became adult in most respects at about age eight, after which they go through a "blackback" period. Although sexually mature, they are not socially mature, do not lead groups, and are still playful.

Infant gorillas weigh 3–5 pounds (1.3–2.25 kg) at birth and stay with their mothers for two to three years, nursing all the time. They are introduced to solid foods at about six months.

Infants nurse almost constantly their first few months, clutching their mothers belly-to-belly. Even when they can walk, they usually stay within a few feet of the mother.

This juvenile mountain gorilla playing with a stick demonstrates the imaginative play of young gorillas, who have been known to play with each other and with their parents. They are not content to just run and climb, but even create games involving round fruit and other vegetation.

An adult male gorilla drives off a young male, as the result of competition for females in the group. Young males (blackbacks) often form "bachelor" groups, until they find available females with which to form new bands.

Once weaned, they also begin building their own nests at night.

For the first few months, infants are totally dependent on the mother, who clutches them belly-to-belly for the first two months. By this time the babies are strong enough to cling by themselves—usually upside down—by holding onto the mother's long chest hairs. After another few months they may also be able to crawl. After four to eight months, the mother carries the baby dorsally, lifting it onto her back to ride with its hands and feet clinging to her hair. The infants may also be able to walk by then, but usually stay within a few feet of the mother. They begin wandering among the other members of the group when they are about a year old.

The mother and her offspring practice grooming, and occasionally a female will groom the silverback, but grooming is not as common among gorillas as among other primates.

Grooming reinforces social bonds and helps clean the fur of dirt and parasites. Bonding assures that the young gorillas learn from their bands to find food, make nests, take care of babies, and get along with other gorillas.

Young gorillas, even some young-at-heart ones, incorporate play into their lives much the same as humans do: chasing each other, wrestling, sliding down trees, playing catch with round fruit, imitating each other, and "dressing up" in leafy vegetation. Mothers have been observed holding their babies over their heads, making them chuckle. (This also sometimes serves the purpose of allowing the infants to relieve themselves in the air and on vegetation, not on the mother's chest.) Even the silverback may allow kid gorillas to crawl all over him and tease him. Silverbacks have even been observed tickling young gorillas, and playing with and petting other small animals.

FOLLOWING PAGE: Infants cling to their mothers' bellies and nurse the first few months of their lives. By the time they are four to eight months old they are able to ride on her back to be carried from feeding stop to feeding stop.

Females breed only once every four to eight years, and produce only one baby. Half of those conceived die in the first year of life or before reaching sexual maturity, due to injury, illness, or dependency on the mother, who also faces these risks.

A group of gorilla youngsters swing on the vines in their jungle habitat, probably creating some game as they go along, or just enjoying the freedom.

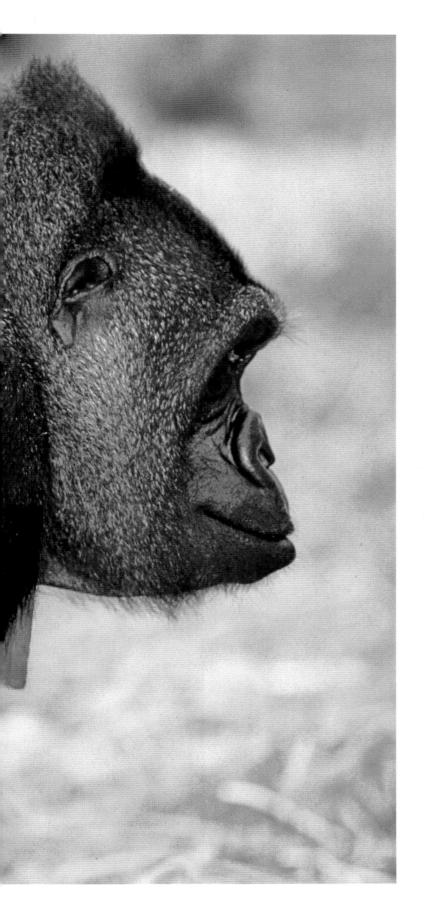

Two young gorillas appear to be play-fighting, which can incorporate chasing, wrestling, sliding down trees, playing catch with round fruit, imitating each other, and "dressing up" in leafy vegetation.

Grooming, which reinforces social bonds and helps clean the fur of dirt and parasites, is not as common among gorillas as it is among other primates. The mother and her offspring practice grooming, and occasionally a female will groom the silverback.

A young lowland gorilla clings to its mother's back as she strolls along. Bonding assures that the young gorillas learn from their bands to find food, make nests, take care of babies, and get along with other gorillas.

Communication

Gorillas communicate with sounds, gestures, body postures, facial expressions, chestbeats, drumming, and odors. They produce more than fifteen sounds, including grunting, coughing, huffing, purring, rumbling, barking, hiccuping, burping, growling, and beating on the chest with open cupped hands, not fists. Yet, unlike chimpanzees, which are relatively noisy, gorillas are quite silent, the gentle giants of the animal world.

Although burping and belching are mostly involuntary during feeding or to show contentment, most of the sounds are used to communicate with the other members of the band. Because gorillas spend a lot of time in high vegetation looking for and eating food, they need to be able to make noises to locate each other and warn of danger or other situations.

Purring, as in cats, shows contentment or happiness, often when eating a favorite food. Grunting is the first line of defense to establish dominance, including right-of-way and settling disputes. Coughing or barking might show that a gorilla is upset or warning about something. "Laughter" sounds like a rumble,

Gorillas use more than fifteen sounds to communicate with each other, including grunting, coughing, huffing, purring, rumbling, barking, hiccuping, burping, growling, and beating on the chest.

A young gorilla is observed "smiling" while swinging from a branch and holding leaves in its mouth. Gorillas are also able to exhibit a range of human-like emotions: They can appear happy, sad, silly, bored, upset, or affectionate.

a softer version of a human ha-ha, almost the sound associated with someone who is hyperventilating. Gorillas also communicate with facial expressions: lip-tucking to show tension, a protruding tongue to show concentration, yawning to show stress, wide open mouth or smile to show playing.

Although the silverback is the gorilla most likely to be seen chestbeating in any group, juveniles also chestbeat as part of their play, and even babies learn to mimic the behavior.

Infants, not surprisingly, have the all-too-human ability to whine, cry, and "giggle" long before they are able to make the usual mature gorilla sounds. But they rarely need to make their needs known since the mother is usually so close by.

Many gorillas also perform chestbeating, for warning, showing off, or just because it feels good. Although the silverback is the most likely to do so (after all, he's the one with the most to be happy about, since he's in charge), juveniles chestbeat as part of their play and even babies learn to mimic the behavior.

Aggressive Behavior?

These sounds and behaviors all seem so docile, yet aren't gorillas usually portrayed as aggressive? Despite their reputation, gorillas exhaust many other means of defense before they attack, which is in itself a rare occurrence. They will put on a noisy display to scare off an attacker or allow the band time to escape, but they do no not attack unless directly provoked. Even then they are most likely to strike or bite, or use chestbeats and postures to ward off an enemy, before resorting to actual attack. In fact, there are no documented cases of a gorilla killing or permanently injuring a human.

Even when silverbacks chestbeat, the behavior rarely develops into a confrontation. Serious fights occur only when a silverback meets another band leader. In these cases,

Gorillas try to ward off an enemy by roaring, growling, staring, head jerking, lunging, grabbing, and biting.

Stalks of bamboo go flying as Mrithi, a silverback mountain gorilla crashes through the brush during a characteristic side charge.

even other members of the group, including offspring, are in danger of being hurt or killed. In fact, when silverbacks fight over a female, her offspring may be killed, and in response she will mate with the killer. However, the killer will then become a devoted father to any resulting offspring.

More often, gorillas try to ward off an enemy by roaring, growling, staring, head jerking, lunging, grabbing, or biting. When a gorilla goes into the ritual charge display, the following sequence of events occurs: hooting, symbolic feeding, standing erect, throwing vegetation, chestbeating, kicking, sideways running (either two-legged or four-legged), slapping and tearing vegetation, thumping the ground.

Etiquette

So now it's clear that gorillas aren't intentionally aggressive. But isn't it possible humans can somehow "set them off" by making what they consider a "false move?" The answer is yes—because gorillas live in a group, much like human societies, they have certain standards of behavior, their own version of etiquette or manners.

For example, gorillas might do things humans don't approve of in social groups, like pick their noses, groom themselves or each other, or use wherever they are as a bathroom. Although gorilla society finds those things are acceptable, other behaviors are not. It is not good to make loud noises or fast, sudden movements, which may make a gorilla feel threatened. So might staring, pointing, chestbeating, or showing one's teeth.

Although it is not considered aggressive behavior, laughing at a gorilla might hurt his "feelings." Instead, be quiet and make no sudden moves; if a gorilla looks at you, nod and lower your head, look away and then slowly look back; crouch or kneel so the gorilla is above or across from you (like curtseying); stay put and observe quietly; if you must smile, don't show your teeth, and try to nod. And whatever you do, don't interfere with their offspring.

Although this vocalizing mountain gorilla appears to be quite fierce, he may just be putting on a noisy display to scare off an attacker or allow the band time to escape, but gorillas do not attack unless directly provoked.

This mountain gorilla manages to get around on all fours even without its right hand, which is missing because of a poacher's snare.

Intelligence

It's obvious that gorillas have some form of what humans call intelligence, defined as "the capacity to acquire and apply knowledge . . . the faculty of thought and reason." Gorillas seem to be able to learn. As infants they follow the leads of their older band members. Some of what they acquire may be based on instinct (an innate knowledge, such as human infants knowing to suckle at birth), but researchers say gorillas, among all the great apes, exhibit a capacity for complex learning. It is estimated that their intelligence is that of a human preschooler, with the absence of language skills, of course. And they are able to exhibit a range of humanlike emotions: happy, sad, silly, bored, upset, affectionate. They are also able to remember people and each other.

Unlike chimpanzees, gorillas have not been observed making and using "tools," but some in captivity have achieved much in the area of communication, learning sign language, and conveying individual words as well as simple sentences directed at people. Koko, a western lowland gorilla in captivity, broke the language barrier in the early 1970s when she was taught to communicate using the various hand signals that make up American Sign Language, developed for the hearing impaired. She is also able to draw with pencils and crayons, although she cannot write words, and she has learned to use a computer specially prepared with pictures at which she points to convey her message. Like humans, she makes faces and examines her teeth in a mirror, lies to avoid the consequences of misbehavior, knows how others may respond to her actions, laughs at her own jokes, grieves, and can describe her emotions.

Koko now has a "vocabulary" of about five hundred words, has used another four hundred or so, and understands a total of two thousand words spoken by humans. The majority of her conversations with humans are initiated by Koko, and she usually averages three to six words per sentence. Koko tries to teach sign language to other gorillas. And when she doesn't know a word, she invents one. For example, zebras are white tigers; ice cream cone, my cold cup; insult, bad mad you; monster, surprise devil; and ring, finger bracelet.

During an April 27, 1998, Internet "chat" with more than twenty thousand people, she "talked" about people, pets, and other gorillas she has known. She conveyed that she would like to have a baby, that she cannot now have one because she does not live in a band, and asked for food and other items she wants. She even knew that talking about something in the future is "fake," meaning something she does not have now.

Obviously, Koko has the reasoning and capability for learning that is required for some degree of intelligence. In fact, she is learning the letters of the alphabet and can read some printed words, including her own name. She has scored between 85 and 95 on intelligence tests, on a scale on which 100 is normal for humans.

Koko lives with two other gorillas. Michael, born in 1973, uses more than six hundred signs, and Ndume, born in 1981, uses natural gorilla gestures and vocalizations.

Unlike chimpanzees, gorillas have not been observed making and using "tools," but some in captivity have achieved much in the area of communication: learning sign language, and conveying individual words as well as simple sentences directed at people.

ENDANGERED STATUS AND PROTECTION EFFORTS

All gorilla populations are in decline. It is estimated that fewer than 50,000 gorillas remain in Africa. Accurate population estimates are difficult to establish because the range has not been thoroughly surveyed, and various gorilla conservation organizations differ in the numbers they determine.

Population Numbers

Fewer than 100,000 western lowland gorillas are left in the wild, in southeast Nigeria, Cameroon, equatorial Guinea, Gabon, Congo (Brazzaville), and the forested areas of the Central African Republic. About 600 of these gorillas live in zoos today, 300 in the United States.

About 2,500 to 10,000 eastern lowland gorillas are believed to remain in the wild, from Zaire to the west of Lake Tanganyika and Lake Edward. There are fewer than two dozen in captivity.

Only 600–650 mountain gorillas are still in the wild, in two small enclaves from the Virunga Volcanoes and the Bwindi Forest at altitudes of 5,400–13,000 feet (1646–3962 m),

FOLLOWING PAGE: Gorillas live in the rain forests and in the densely wooded areas of equatorial west Africa and east central Africa. The two areas are separated by the 622 miles (1,000 km) of the Congo Basin's tropical forest.

There are fewer than 650 mountain gorillas left in the wild, living in two small enclaves from the Virunga Volcanoes and the Bwindi Forest at altitudes of 5,400–13,000 feet (1,646–3,962 m) on the Zaire-Rwanda border and in Uganda. None are in captivity because they are so rare.

This young mountain gorilla is among fewer than 50,000 gorillas remaining in Africa, although accurate population estimates are difficult to establish because the range has not been thoroughly surveyed, and gorilla conservation organizations differ in their estimates.

on the Zaire-Rwanda border, in Uganda, but none in captivity because they are so rare.

Endangered Species Protection

Through the Endangered Species Act of 1973, the U.S. Fish and Wildlife Service lists and protects all gorillas as endangered. The three subspecies are also protected by strict trade regulations established by the Convention on International Trade for Endangered Species (CITES) of Wild Fauna and Flora, a coalition of 145 countries. These countries act by banning commercial international trade on an agreed list of endangered species and by regulating and monitoring trade in others that might become endangered.

CITES operates through an import-export permit system that is stricter for more endangered species. Animals and plants that require protection are classified into one of three appendices. Gorillas are listed in Appendix I, whose species are endangered and could become extinct if their trade is not severely restricted.

Among the species in Appendix I are all lemurs, apes and many monkeys, most whales, most bears, most big cats, all elephants and rhinoceroses, many hawks and eagles, many pheasants, many parrots, many turtles and tortoises, all seaturtles, and most crocodiles.

Appendix II species are not considered endangered, but may become so if their trade is not regulated, such as all flamingos, hummingbirds, chamelons, tegu lizards, monkeys, whales, dolphins, bears, cats (except domestic), wolves, hawks, eagles, owls, parrots, tortoises, crocodiles, pythons, iguanas, monitor lizards, bird-wind butterflies, cacti, and orchids that are not already listed under Appendix I.

Appendix III species, although also not considered endangered, are under special management in certain specific countries. Examples are water buffalo (Nepal), kinkajou (Honduras), hippopotamus (Ghana), rock dove (Ghana), Russell's viper (India), and walrus (Canada).)

Threats to Gorillas

As with most endangered species, the main threat to gorillas is humankind and human activities, such as poaching (for gorilla meat,

As with most endangered species, the main threat to these unsuspecting gorillas is man and his all-too-human activities, such as poaching (for gorilla meat, known as bushmeat), war, and habitat destruction for tourism, farming, and development.

The goal of legislation to protect gorillas as endangered is to assure that this group of young gorillas in Rwanda, and others, will live out their expected lifespans in their natural habitat.

known as bushmeat), war, and habitat destruction for tourism, farming, and development. Over the years, gorilla populations have decreased in direct proportion to the increase of human activity in their areas. The population of humans in the countries in which gorillas reside is among the fastest-growing populations in the world. As more food, water, and shelter are needed for these people, the gorilla loses portions of its habitat to agriculture and logging.

These human disturbances also drive species such as elephants and buffalo to higher altitudes, where they graze on vegetation normally available to gorillas. As gorilla numbers decline, plant regeneration also is reduced, since not as many gorillas are spreading seeds in their dung as they travel.

Fortunately, gorillas are no longer threatened by demand for gorilla hands, skulls, and other grisly mementos. Poachers used to kill male gorillas for purposes of magic called sumu. Their ears, tongues, testicles, and fingers were brewed into a mixture thought to endow men with the virility of a silverback. Poachers also used to capture infant gorillas to sell to zoos.

Gorillas, including this female mountain gorilla, can rest easy knowing that poaching is not the problem it once was. Poachers in the past would target infant gorillas to sell to zoos.

In the past, poachers killed males to use their ears, tongues, testicles and fingers in a "magic" virility brew. Titus, a male mountain gorilla, would have been one of their targets.

As this gorilla group disperses throughout a field, there is some concern that some groups are reducing their travel into certain areas, which also creates problems with plant regeneration.

These chimpanzees at HELP, a sanctuary for orphaned chimpanzees and gorillas in the Congo, would benefit from the establishment of guarded territories for all great ape primates.

However, as the time of this writing, Rwanda is in the midst of a civil war, and gorillas have been caught in the crossfire, both figuratively and literally. The conflict between two ethnic groups broke out in 1990 and eventually led to the exodus of large numbers of refugees. Other countries of the African Great Lakes—Uganda, Burundi, and Congo—have also seen war since the early 1990s. Although these countries may have commitments to protecting gorillas, when their choice comes down to saving gorillas or saving their people, they may choose on the side of their people. Several mountain gorillas have been killed in Rwanda and Congo, one possibly by a land mine and several others caught in gunfire; other gorillas have been injured or maimed. Violence in the jungles also plays an indirect role against gorillas because it reduces tourism, which contributes greatly to the conservation efforts, but the conflicts have forced suspension of tourism in Rwanda and Congo.

This gorilla moving through water in the Mbeli Bai clearing of Nouabale-Ndoki National Park, Republic of the Congo, demonstrates that gorillas do not always avoid water, as previously thought.

The Rusizi River represents the border between Rwanda and Burundi, and runs along the access road to eastern Zaire and the gorillas in that area.

Renowned Researchers

Most of what we know about mountain gorillas comes from the studies of George B. Schaller and Dian Fossey, both directed by renowned archeologist-paleontologist Dr. Louis S. B. Leakey. Leakey and his son, Richard, are also well known for their Early Man discoveries at Olduvai Gorge in East Africa.

Schaller spent several years on the slopes of Mount Mikeno, conducting the first scientific study of the mountain gorillas' habitat and behavior. As a result of these observations, beginning in the late 1950s, he wrote two books: *The Mountain Gorilla* (1963) and *The Year of the Gorilla* (1964). He later studied other animals as well, including tigers, lions, and pandas, and now serves as director for science for the international program of the Wildlife Conservation Society in New York.

Although Schaller's gorilla findings were the first long-term information available, they were based on observing from afar and didn't include as much on gorilla "society" as was later discovered by Dian Fossey. A native of Fairfax, California, Fossey became interested in gorilla research during a 1963 trip to Africa. She began in Zaire in 1966 with support from the National Geographic Society and the Wilkie Foundation. In 1967 she moved to Rwanda, establishing Karisoke, a research enter in the Parc National des Volcans, between the peaks of Mount Karisimbi and Mount Visoke.

Fossey spent much of her time over an eighteen-year period sitting among and playing with bands of gorillas. Her research reached a milestone in 1970 when one of the gorillas, an adult male she had named Peanuts, became comfortable enough in her presence to touch her hand. She was able to follow almost every moment in the lives of three generations of the family group. She even took in two orphaned gorillas, and at least one night brought a sick one into her bed for comfort.

Fossey began census work of the gorilla population in 1969, using field workers to cover the six Virungas mountains: Mount Mikeno (Kabara), Mount Karismbi, Mount Visoke (Karisoke), Mount Gahinga, Mount Sabinio, and Mount Muhavura. They set up temporary camps in various areas, spending several hours each day exploring every gully, ravine, and slope. They recorded old and new signs of gorillas use, including feeding or nesting remnants, and dung deposits. They were able to relate dung size to the age and

sex of the individual gorilla. Once they found a gorilla group, they made nose-print sketches from afar with binoculars to help identify the members. These were supplemented by notes of observations.

Schaller had estimated there were 400 to 500 mountain gorillas in the Virungas. Fossey's census in 1981 counted 242, revealing a 50 percent reduction in population over a twenty-two-year period. (A recent census in Uganda's Bwindi Impenetrable Forest National Park was aided by DNA testing on hair samples taken from each nest. This confirmed that no groups were counted twice and helped researchers understand the genetic differences between the Bwindi and Virunga populations. The results revealed nearly 300 mountain

Exchanging stares with a gorilla in the rain forest could threaten him and result in aggressive behavior. A better idea is to look down, stay quiet, move slowly, and stay away from the young gorillas.

Lorna Anness, a researcher at Karisoke, hugs a soggy gorilla in 1988. During peaceful times, Karisoke is used as a research base for scientists and students, studying the gorilla, other animals, and the local ecosystem.

The late Dian Fossey, who wrote Gorillas in the Mist, *the story of her life with gorillas, is surrounded in 1979 by one of the mountain gorilla troops she studied in Karisoke, which she established.*

gorillas in that area, bringing the total mountain gorilla population to about 600. This census was performed by the Bronx–Zoo–based Wildlife Conservation Society, the International Gorilla Conservation Programme, the Institute of Tropical Forest Conservation, and the Uganda Wildlife Authority.

In addition to researching, Fossey became the world's most fervent advocate for gorillas after poachers killed one of her favorite gorillas, a young male named Digit. Through publicity in National Geographic magazine, she was able to establish the Digit Fund and dedicated the rest of her life to protecting gorillas.

Fossey returned to the United States in 1980 as a visiting associate professor at Cornell University in Ithaca, New York, and wrote about her experiences in *Gorillas in the Mist,* published in 1983. The book brought even more attention to the gorillas' plight, and was made into a major motion picture in 1986, starring Sigourney Weaver.

After writing the book, Fossey returned to Karisoke to continue her campaign to protect the mountain gorilla, and was murdered in her cabin there on December 26, 1985.

Titus, a silverback mountain gorilla in the Karisoke Research Center, Rwanda, takes a morning rest with his group of females and infants.

Conservation Approaches

Although Fossey herself is no longer among those on earth fighting for gorilla conservation, her work is carried on by the Dian Fossey Gorilla Fund International (DFGFI), based in Atlanta, Georgia. DFGFI takes a multifaceted approach to conservation of the endangered mountain gorilla and its habitat, concentrating on four categories: antipoaching, research, education, and economic development.

When staff members find snares, including any dead animals, they cut them down and take them to the camp, so poachers cannot profit. DFGFI guards also patrol the rain forest despite the war. During peaceful times, Karisoke is used as a research base for scientists and students studying the gorilla, other animals, and the local ecosystem. Remote sensing, in cooperation with Rutgers University and NASA, is being used to map and analyze the area. In partnership with authorities in Rwanda, DFGFI provides local conservation programs to local schools and a university. It also plans programs in the United States and with local teachers. DFGFI encourages and supports local development in the areas of water resource projects, health clinics, and craft and tourist industries. It believed that

Kanzi, a gorilla at the Language Research Center, Atlanta, Georgia, shows the good results of a quiz on comprehension and syntax, using animal toys. Many gorillas have been shown to have what humans call intelligence.

development that includes conservation of the ecosystem will minimize the impact on the mountain gorillas.

Another eminent program, the Mountain Gorilla Project, was initiated in 1978 and in 1991 evolved into International Gorilla Conservation Programme (IGCP), a joint effort between the African Wildlife Foundation, Fauna and Flora International, and the World Wide Fund for Nature-International. It is the only conservation program that works within the entire region where mountain gorillas are found, and the only one to work in partnership with all the protected-area authorities within that region. With this support, IGCP has been able to help control the refugees' use of the park's natural resources and coordinate antipoaching activities. In Rwanda, IGCP has provided financial and technical support and has been instrumental in conservation activities.

While these are the major conservation efforts, many other organizations also offer support, either legislative, financial, or educational, including the World Wildlife Fund (U.S. and International), which works to stop illegal trade and supports IGCP. Gorillas are also included in many other studies and conservation efforts that focus on the entire primate order. One such primate effort is the Great Ape Project, a push from a newly established international group founded "to work for the removal of the nonhuman great apes from the category of property, and for their immediate inclusion within the category of persons." Tens of thousands of humans have signed the declaration, which would eventually set up guarded territories for chimpanzees, bonobos, gorillas, and orangutans to live free.

In an unanticipated turn of events, it is believed that tourism has done more to protect some gorillas than any other conservation efforts. In Uganda, for example, all eleven of the national parks are subsidized by gorilla tourism. Because tourists pay a fee higher in proportion to the income of the natives to visit the mountain gorillas in Zaire, the income to the local area gives the residents an incentive to protect their gorillas, rather than poach them for private collectors or food. Personal visits also change the way people view the gorillas, and result in much broader dissemination of knowledge about their plight.

Gorillas in Captivity

After humans realized that gorillas were in such decline in the wild, they felt justified in capturing specimens to keep in zoos for humans to view and to preserve the species. Although this seemed an admirable goal, it did not always serve the purpose. The capture of one gorilla in a band sometimes led to the slaughter of others in the group. Not all the captured gorillas made it to civilization alive. And deaths in captivity far outnumbered the births of gorillas in captivity.

According to recent online abstracts from the International Species Information System (ISIS), an international nonprofit membership organization that serves almost 500 zoological institutional members from 54 countries, there were a total of 661 gorillas in zoos that report to ISIS: 279 males, 377 females, and five infants of unknown gender. The majority, 654, were western lowland gorillas, four were eastern lowland and three were no subspecies. There are no mountain gorillas in captivity.

Dr. Birutè Galdikas, shown with her daughter Jane and orangutans in Borneo, is the world's leading expert on orangutans and co-founded the Orangutan Foundation UK.

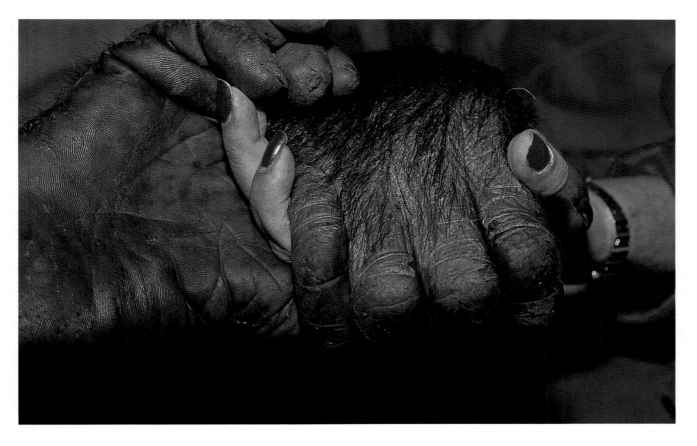

Because gorillas show us they can be almost human—from signing, to laughing, to lying, to loving and grieving—we realize that they are just one step away from being the best of what is human about us.

Gorilla mothers and their infants in captivity are no longer separated, since zoo personnel have learned that infants need to be with their mothers at all times for several years, like this mother and infant in Rwanda.

Silverbacks, reproduction, and infant mortality have been problems in the past for gorillas in captivity, but now gorilla enclosures like this one at Zoo Atlanta, in Georgia, are constructed to meet the needs of gorillas as they would in the wild.

Silverbacks can sometimes cause problems in captivity, since there may be too many dominant males in a small area. Nowadays gorillas may be moved when they reach maturity to prevent such a situation. Bachelor groups of these males are being formed at various zoos all over the world.

As recently as twenty years ago, captive gorillas did not reproduce well. Now that humans understand more about gorilla behavior and provide facilities that meet gorillas' requirements, breeding has been more successful. According to ISIS, there were 33 captive gorilla births in the previous six months. Attacking the reproduction problem from another angle, the first gorilla ever to be produced by in vitro fertilization and embryo transfer was born October 9, 1995, the result of a cooperative project between the Cincinnati Zoo in Ohio, and the Henry Doorly Zoo in Omaha, Nebraska. The resulting female lowland gorilla was named Timi, meaning "team" in Swahili. Another factor in breeding success is that in the past, gorilla infants were often taken from their mothers, but zoo personnel now realize they need to be with their mothers at all times for several years. In addition to being good for the infants, this allows other gorillas the opportunity to learn good parenting skills from one another.

One of the most famous gorillas in captivity is Koko, a western lowland gorilla who became quite famous in the 1970s when she learned American Sign Language and was featured on the cover of National Geographic magazine with her pet kitten. She now lives at the Gorilla Foundation in Woodside, California, in her own specially equipped trailer and two outdoor play areas. Francine Patterson, president of the Gorilla Foundation that serves as a trust on behalf of Koko and the others, is working to establish a preserve in Hawaii, where the gorillas will be able to live semifree in a protected natural environment.

One of Koko's gorilla nieces, Binti Jua, became famous as well, in 1996, when she displayed maternal finesse after a three-year-old boy fell into her gorilla compound at the Brookfield Zoo in Brookfield, Illinois. She picked up the boy and carried him to her keepers to get help for him. Not so public was another incident, in the 1980s, when a little boy fell into the gorilla enclosure at the Jersey Zoo in Great Britain. Jambo, a 400-pound (182 kg) silverback, stroked the boy's back and kept the other gorillas away until rescuers came. Both boys survived, and neither had any injuries caused by the gorillas.

Each band of gorillas favors a certain area within its range and follows a seasonal pattern, depending on which fruits are ripe at a certain time of year. The area each band uses remains fairly exclusive to it, but without territoriality.

INDEX

*Page numbers in **bold-face** type indicate photo captions.*

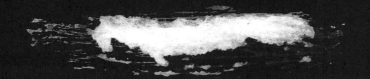